WONDERS OF

THE TREE WORLD

by Margaret Cosgrove

DODD, MEAD & COMPANY

New York

TO MY MOTHER AND FATHER

CONTENTS

A TREE IN A THIMBLE

Whole trees are folded up inside thimbles and in cradles even smaller than thimbles!

An acorn is a thimble with a lid on it. It grows on an Oak tree, and falls to the ground when it is ripe. The autumn leaves cover it up.

The snow falls and keeps the leaves from blowing away.

And the acorn sleeps through the winter, there in the dark.

When the winter is over, the sun grows warm and melts the snow. The rotting leaves from other years have made good soil, and the melting snow wets it. The sunlight warms the soil and touches the acorn.

The baby tree wriggles out one toe and likes what it feels. It reaches out its arms and shoves the leaves away. And it stands in the sunlight and begins to grow . . . and grow . . . and grow . . .

1

ROOTS ARE IMPORTANT

There is just as much of the tree underground as above—a system of dark, mysterious tunnels you might never dream was there.

The next time you see a storm-wind blowing a tree, imagine how deep and firm the tree must anchor its roots in the ground, like long toes, to keep from being pulled up or pushed over. Its toes become miles of claws to hold the earth in place, too. Ground that has no roots in it is blown like desert sand, or is washed away by the rain.

As the root-toes push through the dark ground, so many tiny hairs begin to grow near their tips that they look like velvet. These hairs suck up dampness from grains of dirt that seem almost dry to us, and send the tiniest drops of moisture back along the little roots to bigger roots, until the drops become streams and rivers that flow through the underground tunnels, up and up toward the trunk.

A TREE HAS A HEART, TOO

On the inside a tree is very marvelous—and busy. In the middle is a pole of heartwood. This is hard and helps hold up the tree.

Around the heartwood are many pipes that bring water UP from the roots. There are more of them, and they are much smaller than in the picture. Each year the tree grows a new ring of pipes. When the tree is cut down you can count the number of rings to find out how old it is.

Near the outside is a layer as thin as paper, called the cambium. This is the most important part of the tree because all new pipes grow from it. It is the life of the tree.

Outside the cambium is one circle of pipes bringing food DOWN after it has been made in the leaves.

The bark is wrapped tightly around the whole tree
— to protect the pipes from freezing in winter
— to keep insects and diseases out
— to let air in to the cambium through tiny holes
— to protect the tree from injuries.

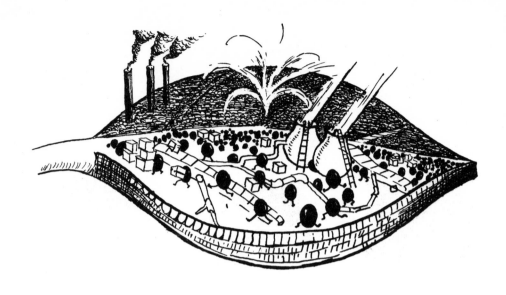

A LEAF IS A FACTORY

Leaves are the greatest factories in the world. No man-made factory can make things the way leaves do, and no one knows exactly how they do it.

Up from the roots comes water that the root-hairs sucked in. Up through the trunk pipelines it rises, and out through the branches and into the leaves. Down onto the leaves comes the sunlight, and through the roof of each leaf-factory, which is as clear as glass.

Inside, the factory is divided into hundreds of tiny rooms, called cells. In the cells are little green workers, packed in so tight the whole leaf looks green. With the water and sunlight they work quickly to make the food — the sap — that is sent out to feed new buds, fruit, seeds, cambium and even the roots.

One thing more the leaf-factory uses—the air we breathe OUT. And we breathe IN the oxygen the leaves make for us. In that way we help the trees and they help us. If all the leaves on earth suddenly died, all the people would die in a very short time!

4

WHY DO LEAVES FALL
IN THE FALL?

Can you guess how green leaves can turn all colors in the autumn?

The leaf-factories work hard all summer, even doing some work at night. Winter is coming and there will be no warmth and little sunlight. The ground will be too frozen for the root-hairs to drink much water. Hundreds of seeds, and perhaps fruits or berries, have been made, and the tree deserves to rest.

The tree has done its work. Back into storage places in the trunk and roots goes the food-sap. Out into the leaves go left-overs the tree hasn't used. Between each leaf and its branch is built a little gateway to close off the pipelines.

It is the left-overs that make the leaves flaming red and golden yellow and deep purple. A leaf, dressed up for its holiday, lets go of the tree and goes sliding down the wind. But even on its holiday it works, for, inside itself, it takes back to the earth the left-overs that will make good soil another year for another tree.

5

TREES IN WINTER

Some people think that trees are more interesting in winter than in summer.

When the leaves are off, you can see that all trees' shapes are different from each other. Thick branches and thin ones, twigs that hang down or curve upward; straight ones, crooked ones. Sometimes many branches come out of a big center trunk, like Sycamore. Sometimes the trunk splits into several big branches, like Elm.

With the leaves off, you can see the witches' brooms in Hackberry and the ruffled seed-cones on Tulip Tree. You can watch squirrels chase each other, and see birds' nests you never knew were there.

Nothing in the world is more beautiful than the lacy, bare trees against the sunset sky on a late winter's afternoon.

HORSE CHESTNUT

TULIP TREE
LEAF EMEMRGING
FROM DUCK-BILL BUD.

COTTON-
WOOD

HORSE CHEST
NUT

MAPLE

WINTER BUDS

When the leaves are gone the tree looks quite dead.
But few people know that before the leaves fell off
they left a promise that more leaves would return
in the spring. The buds of next year's leaves and
flowers are made long before this year's leaves have
fallen. They are small, but are protected by warm
scales. Some are glued together, some are coated
with wax, but all take care of the tiny flowers and
leaves inside them. And in case a late spring frost
should kill the leaves that have started to open, the
tree wears an extra set of buds which will never
come out until it is needed. Here are some especially
interesting buds:

Horse Chestnut's are enormous, black and sticky;
Bitternut Hickory's are golden yellow;
Beech buds are long and pointed, like candle
    flames;
Dogwood has jewel-shaped silver ones.
Watching the fuzzy, sticky, or shiny leaves twist,
shove and unfold in the spring is watching a miracle.

BEECH

AILANTHUS

7

 SUGAR
MAPLE

 CATALPA

BLACK LOCUST

TREE FLOWER GARDENS

PAULOWNIA

It is surprising to know that trees have as many
kinds of flowers as a garden. They are not just to
give pleasure, but to make seeds. The most important parts of a flower are, not the petals, but the
tiny threads in the middle. Several threads that look
alike are called STAMENS, and one that is usually
bigger is called the PISTIL. A tiny box on the end
of each stamen makes yellow powder called pollen.
The pollen falls on the pistil, squirms down the
thread to the bottom of the flower and begins to
make seeds there.

— Sometimes the wind blows the pollen to other
tree flowers.

— Sometimes insects and bees carry the pollen
to other flowers, when they come after the honey
on the pistil.

— Some flowers have beautiful petals to attract
the bees from far away.

— Some have lines on the petals to point the way
inside.

— Some flowers have a sweet smell. Perhaps
people help make seeds by carrying pollen to other
flowers on their noses!

HORSE CHESTNUT

8

PAPER
BIRCH

REMBLING
ASPEN
OTTONWOOD

SWEET
GUM

SYCAMORE

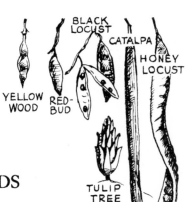

BLACK
LOCUST

CATALPA

HONEY
LOCUST

YELLOW
WOOD

RED-
BUD

TULIP
TREE

KNOW THEM BY THEIR SEEDS

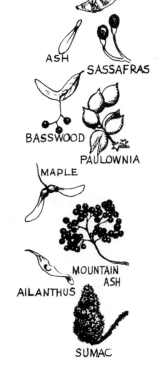

ASH

SASSAFRAS

BASSWOOD

PAULOWNIA

MAPLE

MOUNTAIN
ASH

AILANTHUS

SUMAC

There are more kinds of seeds than anyone could ever invent by himself. Seeds have two purposes: to get places, and to protect the unborn tree inside.

Berries and fruits wear bright colors, so birds and people will see them from far away and want to eat them. Then they can spread the seeds inside to distant places. Good fruit is packed around the seeds, so people will come back for more.

Some seeds spin like propellers, faster than you can watch them; some fly — airplanes can do no better. Some have parachutes or sails for the wind to blow.

Some seeds float on water, some roll downhill.

Some seeds have prickers that stick to dresses, fur, feathers and trousers, to be carried far away.

And some are shot into the air like bullets!

AGE ORANGE

PAWPAW

CRAB APPLE

PAPER
MULBERRY

HAWTHORN

PERSIMMON

WHITE MULBERRY

RED MULBERRY

9

HOW TO FINGERPRINT
THE TREES

Have you ever looked at your finger-tips — closely? Look at your thumb and see the tiny lines that curve into a sort of circle. Everyone in the world has a slightly different pattern — no one in the world has a thumb or fingers marked exactly like yours!

Detectives keep records of people by putting special ink on their fingers and then pressing them on paper. Did you know that *trees* have fingerprints too? And each kind of tree is different from every other kind. Trees' fingers are the leaves with which they catch their food and drink — the sunshine and rain. Like detectives, you can keep records of their fingerprints in a scrapbook. It's lots of fun, and you'll never get them all!

Before you start, tell Mother you'll clean up everything you use. Maybe Dad will help; he'd be good at this. Then get these things ready:

1. A candle, matches and a saucepan with a handle
2. A sheet of paper, some cardboard and a spoon
3. Some leaves that you want to fingerprint
4. A rag and a tiny bit of grease (lard will do)

Put them all on the kitchen table. It's a good idea to spread newspapers on it before starting. Rub some of the grease on the bottom of the pan (outside) and spread it around with your finger. It only takes a little.

10

Ask someone to light the candle for you; and when that is done, hold the handle of the pan with the cloth, in case it should get hot. Now pass the bottom of the pan through the tip of the flame, back and forth, until it is black. When it has cooled off, rub the black onto your finger and then rub it on one side of the leaf.

Now you are ready to take the leaf's fingerprints! Put the black side of the leaf carefully on the white paper and place the cardboard over the leaf. Then rub the cardboard with the spoon, firmly, but not too hard. When you think you've done a good job, lift the cardboard and leaf — and there is the tree's fingerprint! It will take practice to do a perfect one, but keep at it; you can do it.

By the way, find some scouring powder and scrub the bottom of the pan shiny again. It only takes a second and that's fun, too.

THINGS THAT ARE FUN TO MAKE

A scrapbook of real leaves is valuable to make, because you will treasure it when you grow up. Also, it will be fun to add to it all your life. Be sure to pick good leaves that have no holes chewed in them by hungry insects. (If you are on a hike and cannot press your leaf collection right away, put several leaves in a plastic sandwich-bag and close the top tightly. This keeps them from drying out.) To press them, lay them between newspapers and pile a few books on top to keep them flat. At the end of two weeks or more, take them out and place them in your scrapbook, putting scotch tape over the stem and points. Don't forget to write the name of each, where you found it and the date.*

Can you imagine how especially beautiful a scrapbook of autumn leaves would be?

A collection worthy of a museum can be made with parts of trees that can not be pressed. All kinds of Evergreen cones, a Sycamore buttonball, a winged twig of Sweet Gum and a pretty American Hornbeam seed are a few suggestions. Keep them in a box, with cotton or crushed tissue paper packed around them. If you let them lie around the house they will get broken or lost. Museums treat their specimens with great care.

* On pages 14 and 15 you will find silhouette drawings of the most familiar leaves. The numbers refer to the pages where the trees to which these leaves belong are described.

Acorns come in almost as many shapes as people's heads, and you can paint faces on them that will make everyone laugh! You can even create a Nutman from some twigs and two large acorns. Carefully make holes in one that the arms, legs and neck will fit into. Put the face and hat on the other before fitting it on the neck. Some glue or a little melted candle-wax will hold him together. The gentleman in the picture is wearing a mustache made of a Catalpa seed.

A Paulownia or Catalpa leaf will make him a tent to live in. Three twig-poles sewed to the leaf will help it stand up better.

Page 25 tells how to make a Willow whistle. Ailanthus (for city boys) or Basswood can be used also. The wood is easiest to work with in the spring.

A Valentine can be made of a Redbud or small Catalpa leaf, some crayons, colored paper and a paper doily. Of course the leaf would have to be pressed the summer before.

Christmas-tree ornaments that are most unusual can be made of Sweet Gum prickle balls painted bright colors. Coat them with clear nail polish to make them shiny.

THESE ARE JUST A FEW IDEAS.
CAN YOU THINK OF MORE?

13

WHAT TREE IS THIS?

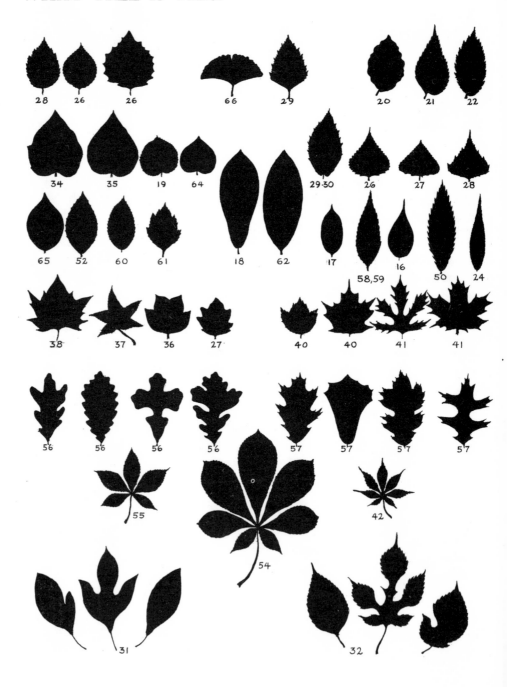

THE NUMBER BENEATH EACH SILHOUETTE TELLS YOU WHAT PAGE DESCRIBES THE TREE TO WHICH THE LEAF BELONGS.

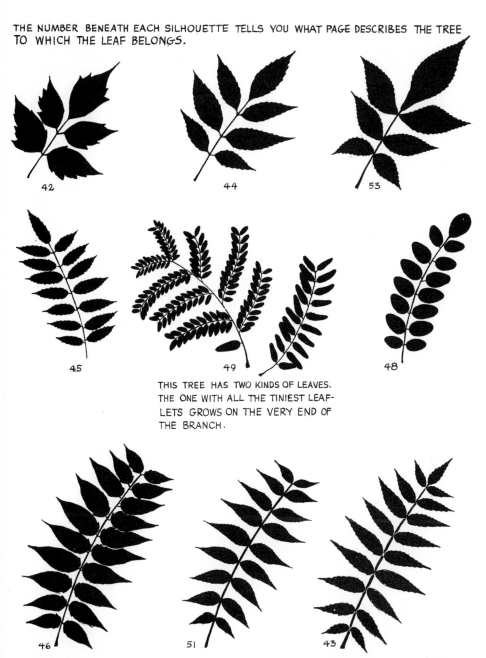

THIS TREE HAS TWO KINDS OF LEAVES. THE ONE WITH ALL THE TINIEST LEAF-LETS GROWS ON THE VERY END OF THE BRANCH.

SOME LEAVES ARE MADE UP OF MANY SMALL PARTS CALLED LEAFLETS. THE LEAVES DO NOT ALWAYS HAVE EXACTLY THE SAME NUMBER OF LEAFLETS AS THEY DO IN THESE PICTURES.

OSAGE ORANGE

This tree first grew in Osage Indian country — Oklahoma and Texas. It has fruit like enormous green oranges, so we call it the Osage Orange tree. It has the best wood for bows, as it's springy and doesn't break easily, so the Indians call this tree Bow-wood. The wood is also harder, heavier and tougher than most other kinds.

Osage Orange has another use now. Through the Middle West, in such states as Illinois, many are planted close together to make hedges with such tightly tangled branches that cattle cannot break through and wander away. The rows make good windbreaks, too, against the winds that howl across the prairies. The roots are such a bright orange color they could never be mistaken for any other tree's. Thorns grow on the branches.

The emerald-green leaves are as pointed as the thorns. The "oranges" are as big as baseballs. And if you don't mind its smell, the milky juice can be rubbed on your skin to keep mosquitoes away; but this ball is much better for rolling down a dusty country road.

PERSIMMON

PERSIMMON is a tree of the South, where the people sometimes call it the "simmon tree." A few grow as far north as New York, Pennsylvania and Illinois. Yellow fruit grows on it, with seeds inside like tiddly-winks. Southern people sometimes play a joke on Northerners by offering them a bite of one, which is so bitter their mouths pucker up so they can hardly talk! But the first touch of frost seems to be magic, and the "simmon apple" turns to sweetness.

People aren't the only ones who like the fruit—after the frost! One animal chooses Persimmon above all others to live in: the opossum. She climbs up the trunk that has bark like a tray of chocolate fudge roughly cut into squares, and makes her home in its branches. Her babies live in her pouch after they are born in the spring, but by fall they are out exploring the tree, even hanging by their tails and getting fat on ripe persimmons. Sometimes this is called the Possum-Plum Tree!

17

PAWPAW

PAWPAW was named by the Indians, but before there were any Indians, it wandered northward from a hotter climate. Its leaves look like tropical leaves; big, soft and smooth. And because they like the heat of summer they become clear yellow in autumn, the color of sunshine.

A hiker, walking through the woods of the Middle West or South, will find Pawpaw colonies, as if the little trees liked just each other's company, with no outsiders. In autumn, a village of Pawpaws, with its golden leaves, looks as though it were trying to hold the summer's sunlight as long as possible in the woods.

Pawpaw's fruit looks like small-sized bananas, only much fatter. Usually they are not good-tasting if they're white inside; the yellower, the better. Some people call them custard apples and like them, but others make a face when they bite into one and say it has the taste of being either not ripe yet or too ripe to eat.

BASSWOOD

BASSWOOD has round leaves that look like balloons with points on them to anyone who gazes up through the branches. Some leaves are lopsided. Some are very fat hearts. And if you study the pattern of the lines in them (the pipelines called veins) you will see how interesting they can be.

No one would ever guess another kind of leaf is there. In spring white flowers hang underneath these special leaves, turning into little hard nuts during the summer. In the fall the leaves come floating down, like peculiarly shaped parachutes, and carry the nuts far enough from the shade of the mother tree so they will have sunlight to grow in.

The wood of Basswood is smooth and white. Wooden bowls, Venetian blinds and strawberry boxes are made from it, and the little sticks the doctor holds down your tongue with when he looks down your throat. In France the peasants made wooden shoes of it, and headache-tea from the flowers. The bees make some of their finest honey from its nectar.

WITCH HAZEL

WITCH HAZEL is a funny little tree that's like a witch who likes to play tricks on people. Her flowers come out in the fall instead of the spring; sunny little flowers with four yellow ribbons for petals that smile through the dismal November woods. Her queerest trick is to *shoot* the seeds out into the woods, with a pop! They're just pea-shooter size.

This small tree has wavy, carefree leaves, a little lopsided. From the bark is made a cool, clear medicine, to rub on sprained ankles and mosquito bites. Is there a bottle on your bathroom shelf labeled "Witch Hazel"?

The reason this tree has such a queer name is that for centuries men called dowsers have believed that a forked stick made from Witch Hazel would twist in their hand as if it were bewitched and guide them in that way to water supplies hidden underground.

HACKBERRY

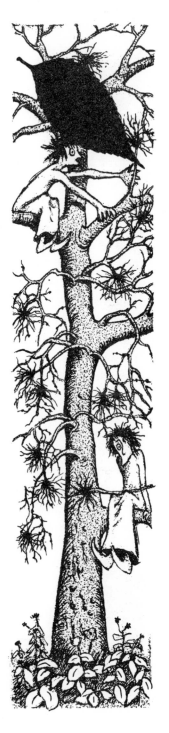

HACKBERRY, like Witch Hazel, knows something about witches, for up in the branches are curious tangles of twigs called witches' brooms! Anyone with imagination will also be reminded of Fourth of July sparklers by them.

Sometimes the light gray bark of the trunk is covered with lumps that look like warts, so you know what tree it is without looking upward. But the witches' brooms are black, and the leaves beside them look very dainty, as if they were made of light green silk. The dark blue berries that ripen in fall are nearly all seed, but what little fruit there is on them is so delicious you wish there were more of it. In the South, Hackberry is called Sugarberry.

Not many people know this tree, but you can find one if you look for it. It's worth finding, with its warty gray bark, its graceful leaves and its curious tangles of twigs. Could this be where the witches get their brooms?

THE ELM FAMILY

AMERICAN ELM looks like an enormous bouquet of flowers in the way it is shaped. After you look at the picture you should be able to see one from a distance and say, "There is an Elm tree!" without even looking at the leaves. No other tree is shaped like it, and it is as easy to spot in winter as in summer.

This big bouquet has flowers in it, as all bouquets do; but what tiny flowers! Remember to look at them early in spring, on the Elm branches that dangle over the sidewalk or out in a pasture. Each flower is as perfect as a lily or violet, with little stamens and a pistil inside.

And then there is SLIPPERY ELM. It is not shaped quite so much like a bouquet, and has larger leaves. Here is another way to tell it from American Elm. Rub your finger over the leaves. American Elm's are rough and fuzzy-feeling one way, but Slippery Elm's are rough both ways, like sandpaper.

Isn't it odd that a tree with such rough leaves should be called slippery? It's because the jelly-like tree food, right underneath the bark, makes the bark slip on the cambium in the springtime when it is touched. Mixed with a little water, this jelly is good for sore throats. People once thought it cured broken bones.

WINGED ELM grows in the South and has wings made of cork on the twigs, like Sweet Gum. It has very small leaves.

CORK ELM grows in the North and Middle West, and sometimes has corky wings to look for, too.

SEPTEMBER ELM is the one that grows in the Mississippi Valley, and it, too, has corky wings.

THE WILLOW FAMILY

Everyone knows the furry "kittens" that grow on Pussy Willow in early spring. But do they know the CATkins on the big Willow trees a few weeks later? These are the trees' flowers, and they look like they had jumped up on the branches to keep their feet dry. For Willows are usually found growing along creeks and in swampy places. They drink so much water their wood is brittle and weak. Sometimes they grow so closely side by side along a brook, they look as if they're trying to hide the water from the sun to keep it cool, or from drying up.

And Willows *swim* to new places! The cottony seeds that come from the catkins in summer land on the water, sprout two little leaves, and drift along like sailboats until their tiny roots catch in the muddy bank somewhere. Twigs and branches break off easily in storms, too, and swim downstream, get stuck in the mud — and grow! Farmers make leafy fences by sticking Willow sticks in the mud.

Each leaf has two little extra leaves on the stem that look like kittens' ears. They usually fall off after the leaves are out, so must be looked for early.

One of the nicest things about Willow is the whistles that can be made from a branch. If tapped gently to loosen it, the inside wood can be twisted out of the bark in spring and a notch cut in one side. Notch the bark too, and then slip the wood back into it and blow!

BLACK WILLOW is the biggest of them all. The bark is dark and rough. A big limb or two usually leans out over the water; it's good to sit on, except that many branches grow out of it and shoot straight upward.

WHITE WILLOW has such flexible small branches, called osiers, that people weave baskets out of them, especially in Europe. The leaves come out next after Pussy Willow in spring and have silvery, silky hairs underneath.

YELLOW WILLOW has another, musical name: Golden Osier Willow, because its osiers are as golden as butter, even in winter.

WEEPING WILLOW is really not weeping at all, but just leaning over to let its long leaf-fingers trail dreamily in the water.

25

ASPEN   BIGTOOTH ASPEN   COTTONWOOD

WHITE
POPLAR

THE POPLAR FAMILY

TREMBLING ASPEN is a tree that twinkles in the sun. The Indians say it is a chatterbox tree. Its leaves have stems as flat as ribbons, and even the littlest breezes are forever shaking them. When the wind blows up the leaves' whitish undersides, farmers note this and "It looks like rain!" they say.

But Trembling Aspen likes the sunshine best. It pops up in a sunny, deserted field, or a place where there has been a forest fire, and makes shade for new trees to grow in. And when the new woods has started growing, Trembling Aspen goes to look for new sun on the edge of the forest, for it can't sparkle its leaves in the shadows. Even its bark is a sunny, light green, almost white. It is the best friend of beavers, for they gnaw it down with their sharp teeth to build their dams. They eat its leaves for salad, and store its branches under the ice for their winter food.

The catkins are especially interesting because they look like long necklaces, for they're strings of tiny flowers in spring. When ripe, each flower has become a little seed pod with cotton in it.

26

COTTONWOOD is beloved as the Prairie Tree. It is one of the few trees that will grow on the prairies of the West. Many people dream of its cool shade on scorching summer days, just as the pioneers did when they crossed America in their covered wagons. Its "cotton" covers the ground and fills the air near and far. On the great prairies and flat lands of the West, this cottony fluff that can ride on the winds is the best way of carrying seeds across the endless miles.

WHITE POPLAR also has cotton, only it grows tight to the leaves and stems, like blankets. It is on the under-side of older leaves, but covers the leaves of young trees and makes them look like ghosts of trees.

LOMBARDY POPLAR is a dignified tree, shaped like a church steeple. It never grows from seeds but from branches stuck in the ground. If a tree is cut down, more trees promptly shoot up out of the trunk, pointing toward the sky.

27

PAPER BIRCH

GRAY BIRCH

RIVER BIRCH

THE BIRCH FAMILY

You would expect a tree that lives in the Arctic Zone to be heavy and sturdy.
But it's the slender PAPER BIRCH that survives there. Instead of being strong
enough to fight the blizzard, it bows to the ground when the winds try to
blow it down. When the storm is over, Paper Birch stands up again, shakes
a little snow from its branches, and sways triumphantly beneath the blue sky.

Paper Birch's bark is as pure and gleaming white as a fishbone. It comes
off by itself in peels, like sheets of paper, and the new bark underneath is
orange until the sun whitens it. To pull it off before it's ready harms the
tree, and may kill it. The Indians made canoes, pails, dishes, shingles and
raincoats from it because it's waterproof and light.

Like Willow, all the Birches have catkins too, only they look more like
CATerpillars. In the spring they whoosh out all over the trees and, when a
breeze takes a puff at them, the *long, fuzzy* caterpillars blow out pollen
dust that catches on the *short, fat* caterpillars, and that's how the seeds begin.

GRAY BIRCH likes to be around people more than Paper Birch does. It springs up like a weed around cities of the Northeast, and in deserted fields. It tries to look like Paper Birch, but is a shade grayer and has big black triangles on the trunk where old branches fell off. The bark does not peel, either.

SWEET BIRCH has twigs that taste like wintergreen! The young trees are satiny red-brown; one of the loveliest surprises in the winter woods. There are little lines and dashes on the bark, so air can reach the cambium. The bark of big, old trees looks like ragged, dull, worn satin; but the little lines are still on it.

YELLOW BIRCH is covered with shaggy, curly strips of tissue-paper bark; some yellowish-gold, some silvery white.

RIVER BIRCH is the only Birch of the South, and has reddish, ragged bark.

29

THE TWO HORNBEAMS

These two Hornbeams are different trees, but they have leaves that look alike. Each tree has two names. The most interesting things about them are their trunk and seeds.

Hop-Hornbeam, or Ironwood, has wood as hard as iron. It was used by the early settlers to make tools, and is still used for that. On the ends of the branches are bunches of little paper bags, each with one seed in it.

American Hornbeam, or Blue Beech, isn't really a Beech at all, although its bark is as smooth and nearly as bluish-gray as a Beech. The trunk is very unusual; it has ridges like the muscles of a strong man's arm. Or you might say it looks as if a ground mole had been running around under the bark, making tunnels. The seeds are in bunches, too, and hang down over the path through the woods. They are. tiny and pretty and don't look quite like anything else at all.

SASSAFRAS

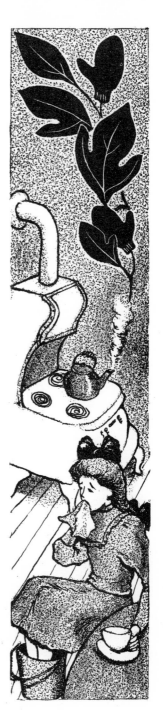

SASSAFRAS is loads of fun. The queer leaves come not only in plain oval shapes but in right-handed mittens, left-handed mittens and mittens with two thumbs! After you've found all four kinds on one tree, break off one and smell the stem. Nothing in the world smells better! You can chew the leaf, too.

Some Sassafras trees are big, but more often they are small and friendly, growing along a path through the woods or in sandy places. The leaves are red in the fall, and the red and blue berries look like little Christmas-tree bulbs.

Sassafras has had a busy life. The early settlers boiled the roots to make a yellow dye for their clothes. The people of London demanded that ship-loads of roots be sent to them for use as a medicine. When Great-Grandma was little and stayed home from school with a cold, her mother gave her sassafras tea, boiled from the roots, which smell every bit as good as the leaves. In the Deep South the Negroes and Creoles dried and powdered the leaves into gumbo soup. And today Sassafras is used to perfume some kinds of soap, but best of all—to flavor gumdrops!

31

THE MULBERRY FAMILY

More than four thousand years ago a princess named Si-Ling-Chi lived in China. Walking in her garden one day, she saw worms on a certain tree, but instead of ordering them killed, she stopped to study them. She saw that they ate the leaves hungrily and then wove threads around them—threads that came out of their heads—to make glistening white cocoons. And she thought to herself that if worms could be clothed so well, what a beautiful robe they might make for her!

And so her people, and later all the people of the Far East, learned to make silk of these threads spun by worms, and they learned to grow the only kind of tree the worms would live in: the White Mulberry. Thirty centuries later two monks smuggled silk-worm eggs to Turkey in hollow canes, and a few hundred years after that, other countries, such as Italy and Syria, were making silk. It was even tried in America around the time of the Revolutionary War, but without much success. Today Japan send us most of our silk — the most beautiful, shimmering cloth in the world, made by worms that eat tree-leaves!

All the Mulberries have queer leaves — three kinds, like Sassafras, on one tree, especially on the smallest ones. And there are three kinds of trees to look for.

WHITE MULBERRY is the silkworm tree and has white berries that the early settlers called "silk seeds." Birds squall with delight at the good taste. The leaves are small, smooth and shiny.

RED MULBERRY drops reddish-black fruit all over the ground. Chickens, pigs and ducks squeal greedily for them and grow fat on them. The leaves are just a little rougher than White Mulberry's, but the silkworms don't like them.

PAPER MULBERRY has fuzzy seed balls instead of berries. The leaves are big, with thick velvet underneath. In many countries people scrape the outer bark with a shell and soak the inner bark in water. Then they beat it on a flat log until it is a beautiful white cloth. In Samoa the natives paint designs on it and call it "Tapa." The Japanese people use it for paper lanterns and umbrellas.

33

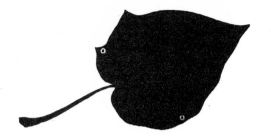

PAULOWNIA

Just as immigrant people have brought good things to America, so have immigrant trees. PAULOWNIA has had a long journey, but we're glad it's here. It has brought us good, light wood that grows quickly. In early June, while the tree is still bare of leaves, lavender flowers, shaped like bells, bloom out. Their picture is on page 8.

This tree was named after a Russian princess, Anna Pavlovna. It was a royal tree in Japanese courtyards, where it was called the Empress Tree. In Japan the wood is good for use in the small, light houses the people must have on these islands that are shaken by tremendous earthquakes.

The leaves are shaped much like Catalpa's but are as wooly as blankets underneath. Paulownia is commoner in the South than the North, and through Tennessee and Kentucky its enormous bunches of wooden seed-boxes hang out over the roads in autumn.

CATALPA

The Indians loved the woodlands and knew them well, and that is why so many trees are named after them. CATALPA was named after the Catawba Indians, even though the spelling was changed somewhere. Catalpa is also called the Indian Cigar Tree, because its long, thin pods look like cigars; but the Indians never really smoked them. The little seeds inside look like mustaches. Notice how its yellowish, smooth bark, sometimes with big lumps on it, is different from that of Maple or Elm.

Catalpa sleeps late in spring, just as Paulownia does, until other trees have nearly finished putting on their new leaves. But when it does awaken it likes to dress itself up. The leaves are so big you can recognize the tree a block away. In June it is heaped with flowers; large, frilly ones that cover the ground when they fall. They have dotted lines to point the way to the center where the nectar is. Insects don't need a second invitation to enjoy the fragrance — nor do people!

Many of the pods stay on all winter. Through wind and storm they sway, like the fringe on the dress of an Indian squaw.

35

TULIP TREE

Tulip Tree is one of the biggest in the woods, for it comes from the deep forests where its immense trunk holds branches and leaves up to the very ceiling of the dark woods. It has good wood — carpenters can make a whole house from just one large tree! Indians used to burn out the inside of a trunk and then smooth it with shells to make a "dugout" canoe.

Tulip Tree has flowers — tulips — sitting on the branches in spring; green tulips with splashes of orange on them, that hold honey like a cup. The leaves are shaped like tulips, too. During the summer the tulips turn into what look like brown, ruffled candles, full of seeds. They fall to the ground in autumn, and you can find them there.

Something to look for is the funny little green buds, shaped like ducks' bills. When they open and a leaf comes out of each one, they turn into little donkeys' ears until they fall off.

In the forest, where everything must be strong or clever to live, Tulip Tree is one of our mightiest kings.

SWEET GUM

This is the tree with the delicious name. In the South, where SWEET GUM is happiest, the gummy sap that flows through its pipelines has a fragrant smell, and some people like it better than chewing gum! It is even used to make perfumes. This sap is stored in the roots and trunk through the winter, and when spring comes it streams upward toward the stars. For Sweet Gum has stars for leaves, dark green stars that flash back the sunlight, just as the sky's stars twinkle in the night.

In the fall the star-leaves turn to deepest red and float away through the air. The golden sap they made through the summer is stored away once more. When the tree is bare of leaves, something unusual can be seen. On some twigs the bark, instead of lying flat, stands on edge, as though it had been carelessly pasted on the wrong way. It looks like three wings, made of cork, standing out.

Sweet Gum protects its seeds well, in the prickliest of prickle-balls. Step on one and see!

SYCAMORE

This tree was made for climbing. If you can get up to the lowest branch, you can walk to the top as easily as going upstairs, and there are no sharp angles to catch your foot in. The branches come out of the trunk almost straight, and are strong nearly out to the end. Look down from the top and see how they come out like the spokes of a wheel.

While you are up there, take a look at the bark. (You can see it just as well from the ground.) No other bark is quite like it, for as the tree grows bigger, the bark bursts and the new white bark underneath looks just like underwear! The tree keeps growing too fat for its clothes, and must grow a new suit every year. But patches of the old one cling to it: rags of green and brown over new, shining white.

The leaf stem hides something unexpected. If it is broken carefully off the branch, a new bud can be seen underneath it. This is Sycamore's way of protecting its buds until they are ready to take care of themselves.

The leaves are big, clean and crisp, making clear reflections in the water along which Sycamore often grows. But late in the fall and all during the winter, when the leaves are gone, near the top of the tree many prickle-balls still hang, like Christmas-tree ornaments. They are also called button-balls, or itchy-balls. When you find one on the ground you can pull it apart and see the many tiny seeds inside it. Each one has a fuzzy parachute for the wind to blow, so that boys far away will some day have more Sycamore trees to climb.

The LONDON PLANE TREE is the city cousin of Sycamore. It doesn't mind sooty air, and its branches are smaller to fit the city streets without being crowded by the buildings. Its bark is a little darker than Sycamore's.

39

SUGAR MAPLE   RED MAPLE

THE MAPLE FAMILY

Maple trees were some of the first American citizens, for just as the Indians were here long before the first pioneers came, Maple was here to greet the trees from other countries. The Maple family is a large one, with members that live in many places.

Maple leaves are shaped like your hand. Some kinds have a V-shape between the fingers, some have a U-shape, as in SUgar Maple. This trick will help you to recognize them. Maple seeds are wonderful airplanes. They are sometimes called Maple keys, and may be the key to finding out the kind of Maple, for each one is a little different. The keys also ripen at different times; for example, Red and Silver Maples in spring, Norway Maple in summer, Sugar Maple and Box Elder in autumn.

One of our favorite members of the family is SUGAR MAPLE. In New England its sap is so sweet that farmers make sugar of it. They put a small spout in the tree in early spring, and the sap, moving up to the new little leaves, drips out into a bucket. The farmer boils it down until he has thick, clear maple syrup; and if he boils it even more, he will have maple sugar!

His children put some syrup on a dishful of snow until it becomes sticky; then they eat it with a dill pickle!

RED MAPLE has some red on it nearly always. Its small leaves have bright red stems where the sun touches them. In spring the thousands of fat, red buds make the tree look lost in a crimson cloud. The keys are red too, and in autumn the leaves burst into fiery red early, as a signal that winter is coming.

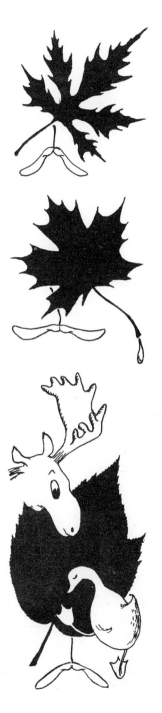

SILVER MAPLE has graceful leaves, with a deep U between the fingers. When the wind blows them up, the silver undersides flash. The wood is weak, so be careful — branches break off easily in storms.

NORWAY MAPLE wasn't here with the Indians; it came later. In spring, covered with yellow-green bouquets of flowers, it stands out from other trees. The leaves are a little like Sugar Maple's, but are larger and darker, and with a secret difference. The stem has a drop of milk inside. Taste it!

STRIPED MAPLE is called this because of the beautiful lines on the trunk and branches — white lines on smooth, green bark. Its leaves, shaped like a goose's foot, are large, but its keys are small. Moose love to eat the bark, and that's why its other name is Moosewood.

41

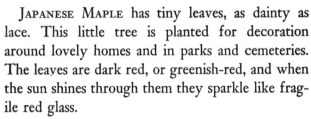

JAPANESE MAPLE has tiny leaves, as dainty as lace. This little tree is planted for decoration around lovely homes and in parks and cemeteries. The leaves are dark red, or greenish-red, and when the sun shines through them they sparkle like fragile red glass.

BOX ELDER doesn't sound like a Maple, and its leaves don't look like a Maple's. But it has Maple keys to prove it is one. It likes the Middle West and South best, from North Dakota to Georgia, and does much good by protecting these states from the sun and wind. The wood is used to make crates, furniture and wooden bowls.

BIGLEAF MAPLE grows out West, in states such as Oregon and Washington. Its leaves are so big that a picture of one wouldn't fit on this page! Such big leaves make the towns cool and shady, and the forests dark and mysterious. The big, fuzzy keys grow in big, fuzzy bunches.

SUMAC

Sumac tries very hard to be an interesting tree, so it won't be blamed for having so many poisonous relatives: poison ivy, poison oak, poison sumac. But know Sumac for itself; it can't help who its relatives are.

In far-away Arabia Sumac was given its name. And because of the fuzzy, velvety branches like the horns of a stag, we call it STAGHORN SUMAC. This is just a little tree with wood not good for anything, that likes sunny openings in the woods or to stand beside the road and watch the cars go by. The leaves, made up of many small parts called leaflets, are the brightest of all reds in the fall. And held up proudly are the piles of fuzzy red seeds, as velvety as the branches. Perhaps it was the American redskins who discovered that a drink could be made from these red velvet seeds called—Indian lemonade!

Remember: Poison Sumac has *smooth* branches and green berries, *white* when ripe.

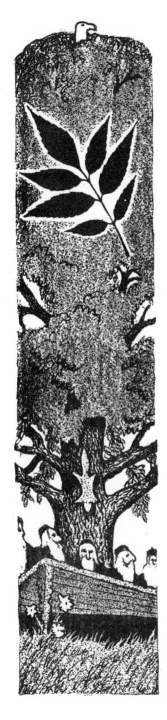

WHITE ASH

Ash is modest and quiet. It doesn't wave big flowers in the spring, or have queer bark, or unusual leaves. It's just a quiet, respectable tree.

Yet they sing about it in Ireland, and it was once said in Scotland that its morning and evening shadows killed snakes. The Scandinavians have a very old poem that says the court of the gods is under an Ash tree, whose roots are in the underworld and whose top branches are in heaven. An eagle sits in the top and sends down messages by a squirrel, of all the world's happenings that it sees.

White Ash has many sisters and brothers: Green, Blue, Red and Black, but they all look quite a bit alike. Don't get the leaf mixed up with that of Hickory. The fine wood of the Ash makes ax handles, baseball bats and tennis rackets. Its seeds are the tongues of birds, the people of Europe sometimes say. But we say they look like canoe paddles. Maybe they are the tree's way of remembering how the Indians used to make their paddles of its fine wood.

MOUNTAIN ASH

If you look in the telephone book, you will probably find lots of people with the same name as yours, but no relation to you at all. MOUNTAIN ASH has the same last name as White Ash, but is no relation either. The birds have no trouble telling the difference, for, although the berries are not good-tasting, their bright orange color shining across the snow in winter is like a welcome flag signaling the hungry birds.

These big clusters of fiery berries decorate the tree so brightly that people like to plant Mountain Ash along sidewalks and in parks, where it can be admired. The leaves frame the berries with such lacy foliage they make the little tree look dressed up for Sunday all week long.

Mountain Ash changed its name in America. In Scotland, Ireland and Wales it is called the Rowan Tree, and the people used to tie branches of it over the barn door to scare away witches and lightning from the cows!

AILANTHUS

This is the backyard tree. Its roots burrow under fences and through sidewalk cracks and find food where other trees would starve. Its branches reach up behind buildings, searching for sunlight in the dirty city air where no other tree could breathe. But AILANTHUS likes it!

Each spring hundreds of city people watch the leaves push out from round buds, which are only at the ends of branches. As they watch the leaflets unfurl they wonder how so many could possibly fit into such a small bud. Something to look for is the little bumps on each leaflet, which smells like newly mowed grass when you crush it in your fingers.

The seeds are little airplane propellers. Late in fall they whirr through the air and into cracks in brick walls, or a little dirt under a fence, or even onto a roof, until it is time to begin growing the next spring. Maybe that is why Ailanthus' other name is Tree of Heaven, because it brings beauty into places that would be ugly and barren without it.

CHINABERRY

CHINABERRY does for the country what Ailanthus does for the city. It makes cool, shady places in the hot South, and is especially welcome when it springs up on dry, sun-baked land. It is like an umbrella that keeps the sun off the earth; in fact, they call it the Texas Umbrella Tree in Texas. Insects don't like the wood, so it is good to use for such things as boxes and closets.

Chinaberry started out being an umbrella tree in hot, dry Persia, where it was called *Azad-darach*. But it has many other names too; its light purple flowers give it the name of Persian Lilac. (Lilac is that big bush everyone knows that is covered in spring with cones of purple or white flowers.) In India people give Chinaberry flowers to show their thanks, instead of just saying thank you. It has another name: Bead Tree; and in case you are wondering why it's called Chinaberry, the reason is that the shiny seeds, so many they weigh the branches down, look like China beads and people of many countries string them into necklaces.

47

BLACK LOCUST

BLACK LOCUST has thorns like thumbtacks. It has rough, dark old bark with deep ridges that look like mountain ranges and canyons. It is one of the best trees for twisting its strong roots into the earth, to keep the soil from washing away where men have not taken good care of it. The wood is very hard and lasts nearly forever. And so anyone would expect dark, rough old leaves; but here is a great surprise. The leaflets are tiny and a beautiful color of green. Looking up through the tree, you see lacy, airy foliage that floats softly on the wind. But if a storm is coming up or the sun is setting the leaflets slowly close, like babies folding their hands in the evening.

Late in spring, when Black Locust finally begins to come out, wreathes of sweet-pea flowers dangle from it. When they drop they look like showers of fresh popcorn. The Indians say a squaw in the sky slices off pieces of the moon and throws some out to become stars and others to become Black Locust flowers. They bring heavenly fragrance with them.

HONEY LOCUST

HONEY LOCUST has thorns with thorns on them!
Dangerous daggers they are; sometimes a long one
has five or six daggers growing out of it. They are
in bunches on the trunk and branches, but sometimes thornless trees are grown in parks so no one
can get hurt. The bark, though brown, looks like
butter spread quickly on bread with a knife.

There is an extra-large leaf on the end of each
branch (see the picture on page 15). The leaves
are made up of little bean-shaped leaflets. There are
beans, too, in the long, curling pods. And here is
Honey Locust's surprise: there is more sugar in this
tree than in Sugar Maple, if anyone cares to look
for it! The pods have sweet pulp inside, and the
beans can be ground up to make a drink like cocoa.
Cows love the pods—a farmer reported that his
cattle broke down fences to get at a tree. Who
knows, some day Honey Locust may give us a new
and favorite food!

In the winter the pods rattle noisily when they
blow across the snow. They are probably trying
to get people to notice them.

THE LEAVES ARE MADE
UP OF MANY LEAFLETS

THE PODS HAVE SWEET
PULP INSIDE

BUT NOT ALL HONEY LO-
CUSTS HAVE THORNS.

49

THE NUT TREES

Everyone loves to sink his teeth into the hard, white meat of a nut. Animals and birds crave them as much as humans do. So the trees protect their nut-children by making them green while the leaves are green and turning them brown when the leaves turn brown. (Notice that nut trees usually don't have autumn leaves of red or yellow.) The color hides them, but the nuts themselves are fighters. They are woody and hard to open, and some have husks with prickles on them. They are good at rolling downhill, or even floating along streams, so that new trees can grow up in new places.

CHESTNUT is a treasure to be looked for. Boys and girls in days gone by used to gather its delicious nuts in the autumn, but a disease has killed nearly every Chestnut tree. Little trees still begin to grow and wave their saw-toothed leaves, however, and we hope a cure for the disease will be found before they, too, die.

BEECHNUT   BUTTERNUT   HORSE CHESTNUT and BUCKEYE

ACORN

CHESTNUT   WALNUT IN THE HUSK   HICKORY NUT

BLACK WALNUT

Dent-soo-kwa-no-ne is what the Indians called this tree. It is a fine old American, famous for its wood, which is used for outstanding carvings and furniture. Greedy people have cut down most of the oldest trees; we hope they will give the ones that are left a chance to grow big.

It is second most famous for the walnuts it bears. The husks are knocked off with a hammer and the inside is laid in the sun to dry. Fingers will be stained with brown, but it's worth it for the tangy smell of the juice and, later, on a cold winter night, for the taste of the nuts themselves when they are shelled and eaten. We call this tree BLACK WALNUT —easier to say than *Dent-soo-kwa-no-ne!*

BUTTERNUT looks much like Black Walnut, but the buttery nut is locked in a sharp, tighter shell. A picture of the nut is on page 50.

BEECH

BEECH is a no-other-like-it tree. One could almost say there are two kinds, the field Beech and the forest Beech. The field Beech grows where it has room to spread out its branches, and has smooth, gray bark that looks kneaded and gnarled, like a handful of modeling clay. The forest Beech is exactly the opposite. The trunk shoots straight upward, like a pillar of steel.

Beech has most unusual buds, long and pointed. All winter you can see them, shaped like candle flames, on the branches. In spring the opening leaves spray out, covered with long, silver hairs. Their beauty makes people stop and stare. In the autumn birds and chipmunks love the little triangle-shaped nuts, *after* the prickly husk has burst open.

Our word "book" came long ago from the German word "buche," which means Beech tree. Here is the reason: before there were printing presses or even paper, men wrote their "books" on slabs of Beech tree wood.

HICKORY

Now here is a tree that might once have been your enemy, and with good reason. Teachers used to make stinging switches of it for spankings—at least the song "School Days" says so. But teachers don't do that any more, so let's be friends with Hickory. It grows in no other country than the United States and Canada.

There are several kinds, but the leaves are all very much alike. An old SHAGBARK HICKORY has bark, as tattered as the shingles of a haunted house ready to fall down. But don't let its shaggy bark fool you; the wood is much too strong and tough for Hickory to collapse. Its nuts are so good that not only do squirrels love them, but the Indians used to mash them into white, milky juice for drinking.

—BITTERNUT has gold winter buds and velvety stems in summer.

—MOCKERNUT's stems are hairy and have a nutty smell when crushed.

—PIGNUT has smooth leaves and stems.

53

HORSE CHESTNUT

HORSE CHESTNUT has the size and strength of a horse. Farmers used to say the nuts were only fit for horses; but they are bitter, and although deer eat them if they're hungry enough, horses think even less of them than deer.

By late summer the leaves have grown to a large size and feel nearly as leathery as a horse's hide. They remind you of beach umbrellas. Each one is made up of six or seven leaflets, joined together in the middle, to meet the stem of the "umbrella." In the winter the buds are the most noticeable of all the winter buds. They are big, black and sticky, standing up on the ends of the thick branches. Where the leaf-stems fell off, scars were left that look like horseshoe marks on the bare branches.

This isn't the kind of tree anyone would expect to cover itself with dainty pink and white twin-flowers in May. And in the fall, from inside frighteningly prickly husks come nuts that are as shiny and polished as the coat of a thoroughbred horse.

BUCKEYE

If Horse Chestnut is fit only for horses, as the farmers say, the BUCKEYE nut isn't even good for them. The two kinds look alike: round, shiny and brown, with a gray circle on each. When the shell is half-open it looks a little like the eye of a buck (a big father deer), and that's how it gets its name. Boys and girls who live in Ohio know their state is called the Buckeye State, and they like to find a buckeye and put it in a pocket to carry around.

The leaves look a lot like pinwheels on the Buckeye tree. The roots can be used to make soap, and it is said that the leaves, with a little water, make a soapy lather too, but you'll have to try it yourself to make sure. The nuts are dangerous to eat, but the Indians had a use for them. By a special process they made a "medicine" of them and spread it on a stream. The fish were put to sleep by it and floated to the top, where the Indians scooped them up with no trouble at all! The law forbids this now and, besides, the Indians have probably all forgotten how.

WHITE OAK   CHESTNUT OAK   POST OAK   BUR OAK

THE OAK FAMILY

Of all the trees, the OAK tree is the old grandfather, strong and dependable. Half the dead leaves hang on all winter, just like Grandad's beard, and they rattle in the chilly winds.

It's easy enough to recognize an Oak, but to know the two kinds is harder. They are Grandfather White's and Grandfather Black's families.

White: 1. Leaf fingers are rounded and smooth.
       2. The bark is light-colored.
       3. No acorns on the tree in winter.
Black: 1. Leaf fingers have tiny points, like claws.
       2. The bark is dark.
       3. Half-ripe acorns on the tree in winter.

The acorns are the Oak's seeds. They look like little cups and saucers.

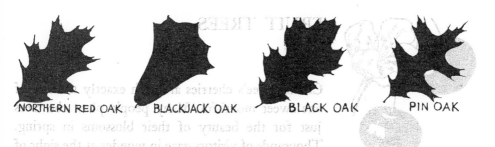

NORTHERN RED OAK   BLACKJACK OAK   BLACK OAK   PIN OAK

If it weren't for the squirrels, there might not be so many Oak trees, even though they do eat a lot of the acorns. The bushy-tails race through the dead leaves on the ground, eating some acorns and burying others for the winter months ahead — and then they forget where they buried them! But burying them is planting them, and new Oak trees are born, all because the squirrels have poor memories. Not only squirrels but thousands of people have lived on acorns for thousands of years, and, in some places in the world, still do. Acorn mash is oatmeal, bread and potatoes for these people. Racoons, bears and hogs know what is good, too, when they search for White Oak acorns.

There are many things to notice about the Oaks. In spring the catkins hang on the trees like tassels. Watch for the opening leaves that look like tiny, pink-velvet baby blankets. Look at your dining-room table, and if it is as polished as a dark mirror, find out what kind of wood it is. Some of the most beautiful furniture in the world is made of sturdy Oak wood.

FRUIT TREES

CHERRY tree's cherries are each exactly the size of one sweet mouthful. Many people plant the trees just for the beauty of their blossoms in spring. Thousands of visitors gaze in wonder at the sight of hundreds of trees in Washington, D. C., sent to us as a gift by the people of Japan. The bark is smooth, dark-red satin, especially up in the branches.

There are plenty of WILD CHERRY trees, too. The cherries are littler and not as sweet, but delicious to find in the woods, if there are any left after the birds find them. Some wild cherries are red, some black.

PEACH tree has big, fuzzy fruit. The flowers are pink and by themselves along the twigs, instead of in bunches. The pit has poison in it, but the firm, pink-and-yellow fruit is delicious and healthy.

PEAR tree has the juiciest, drippingest of fruit. Its blossoms, like Apple's, usually grow on spurs—short branches a fourth of an inch long, that look like tight little springs.

OLIVE tree has the most curious-tasting of all fruit. It grows in orchards in the West, but sometimes the trees escape and become wild. So long ago that no one remembers when or where, men gave olive oil as peace offerings; later they gave a sprig of Olive leaves instead. Pictures of the American Eagle often show him carrying an olive branch as a sign of peace.

QUINCE is the forgotten tree; few people know of its possibilities or strange beauty. It is a little, twisted dwarf that bears fruit too bitter to eat raw. But the golden quinces make delicious jam and marmalade, and the way the blossoms unroll is one of the miracles of springtime beauty.

PLUM tree's blossoms are small and greenish white, but the fruit is red, purple, green, blue, or yellow. When plums are dried they become prunes. The Plum tree, say the Japanese, is the bravest of all trees because it has the courage to blossom before the snow has melted.

APPLE CRAB APPLE

APPLE TREE

Our favorite APPLE tree is like a pet that lives in the backyard. It gives us one of our most delicious foods, but we take it for granted. Let's see how faithful it is.

Thousands of years ago, wild Apple trees covered the slopes of the high Caucasus Mountains in Russia with white blossoms. When some of the mountain people left their homes, they took the best seeds with them. They moved across country after country in Europe, and always Apple went with them. Hundreds of years later, Europeans crossed the Atlantic Ocean to the New World, bringing seeds with them. And in America, a young man raised Apple trees because he loved them, and then spread the seeds across the states among the pioneers. Farther and farther west he went, and the pioneers and Indians called him "Johnny Appleseed," and sent word ahead that he was coming. And so by the time he reached the West he was a gentle old man.

Finally Apple trees reached the Pacific Ocean, and crossed it. The Japanese people love it today for its fragrant blossoms. Someday faithful

Apple tree may cross the rest of Asia and finish its trip around the world, when it comes home to the Caucasus Mountains.

Apple tree never complains about the cold, but becomes sick and dies when it lives in warm southern climates. It likes hard times. Its branches are strong and gnarled so storms cannot break them. The cool, sweet, crunchy fruit hangs on branches too short and stubby to break under the weight.

CRAB APPLE has little, sour apples on it, but animals come out of the woods to find them. Sometimes it grows in pastures or in the gardens of old, deserted farmhouses. The fragrant blossoms, like Apple's, are rose-colored on the outside, and the fallen petals cover the ground like snowflakes.

BLOSSOM TREES

HAWTHORN has such a large family no one is quite sure how many members are in it. All the kinds have slightly different leaves. It gets its name from its little red fruits, called haws, and from the thorns it usually wears.

SHADBLOW is like a cloud of soapsuds in spring, on rocky hillsides and beside pasture fences. Its other name is Juneberry, because the berries can't wait until fall to ripen. They are so delicious they are sometimes called sugar-plums!

YELLOWWOOD is actually a member of the pea family, and even has pods on it. The bark is as light gray as that of Beech, but the heartwood is so yellow it will turn water yellow. It has another name as pretty as the tree itself: Virgilia.

SOURWOOD grows in the South, too. The long sprays of pink and white flowers are dainty in the springtime, and colorful in the autumn when the flowers have turned to red seeds. The leaves are first of the trees to turn crimson at a touch of cool weather.

MAGNOLIA has the queen of the tree flowers. The blossoms, pink or white, are sometimes as big as cups. Magnolia is famous for growing in the South around old colonial homes, but many grow farther north, sometimes in swamps, and are big trees of the forest.

The leaves of some kinds of Magnolias are very large and are velvety underneath. The red seeds are in queer pods and hang out on threads when they are ripe. See page 14 for a picture of the leaf.

FRINGE TREE's flowers are like the fringe around an old-fashioned lace curtain, but they also remind you of something that gives them another name: Old Man's Beard! The berries look like blue olives.

SILVERBELL's flowers are white bells. Some people call this the Snowdrop Tree. It blossoms early, as if to ring in the news that spring is here.

63

REDBUD

REDBUD steals the show in the spring. It bursts into bloom like a pinkish-purple ballet dancer. The whole tree is covered with blossoms; not just single ones or in clusters, the way tree flowers usually grow, but they grow from the twigs and branches and even the trunk. They look like tiny bonnets.

At the end of the twigs the little leaves begin, making the tree into a pink-and-green ballet dancer. As the leaves grow bigger, they become perfect valentine-hearts! Everything about the tree is dainty; even the seed pods are rosy pink.

Some people in Canada eat Redbud flowers in salad, and some fry the pods while they are young and tender, for a delicate food. But most people like best just to admire the valentine-dancer, celebrating spring on the edge of the woods or on a green lawn.

DOGWOOD

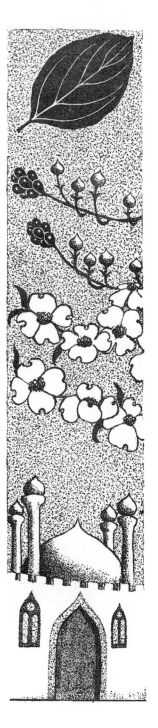

Dogwood has all the pureness of Easter, the cleanness of spring and the freshness of hope. It shows how a tree can look dead all winter, but still hold in its buds a promise that it is not dead but will bloom again, covered with layers of white flowers held up to the sky.

It is surprising to examine one of the white flowers and find many tiny yellow flowers in the center. You can examine the slender trunk, too, and see how hard it is. The Indians used to make spears of it. Some people in the United States and Canada used to fray the twigs to make toothbrushes, to clean and polish their teeth. The roots can be boiled to make a bright red dye for clothes.

But even in the fall and winter Dogwood is beautiful. The red dye hidden in the roots paints the berries so they sparkle like rubies. And the twig-tip holds up jewelry of silver—the most beautiful of all the winter buds. These are the promise that nothing ever really dies. These are the promise that this winter, too, will pass, and spring will come again. It is the most important promise in the world.

GINKGO

GINKGO has the strangest of all leaves, and is the strangest of all trees. It grew on earth millions of years ago, long before there were any people at all, long before there were even any of the kinds of animals we have today. Dinosaurs, the largest land animals that ever lived, paced through the Ginkgo forests, and queer birds flew among the trees.

But slowly the earth grew colder and the great dinosaurs died, and then the Ginkgos began to die, too. Thousands of years passed, and new kinds of trees were starting to grow instead, but no Ginkgos. Only, that is, a very few that managed to hide out in a small, warm valley in China. After millions of more years their children-trees began to spread through China again, and after many centuries more,

66

some were brought to America. Now they stand along sidewalks and in parks, looking down on very different kinds of animals than their ancestors saw so long ago.

Ginkgo leaves are shaped like Chinese fans. The branches are wrapped around with garlands of leaves, for there are no small twigs on Ginkgo. Sometimes a branch shoots out from the trunk as though it were on the wrong tree by mistake. Some of the leaves have a slit in them, like a slice of pie cut out. It is the leaf *fossils* that tell us how long ago Ginkgo lived. A few leaves that fluttered to the ground those millions of years ago fell on mud or clay that, through the ages, turned to stone. But the print of the leaf was left, and in these stone fossils we have as clear a record as that made by a footprint pressed in the wet cement of a new sidewalk.

Look long at this tree, and think of how old the world is and how it changes. Ginkgo will watch many more changes come over it.

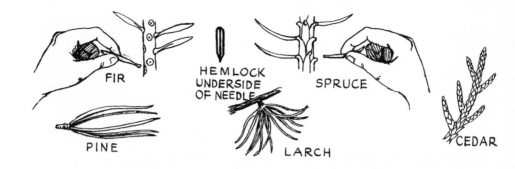

FIR

HEMLOCK
UNDERSIDE
OF NEEDLE

SPRUCE

PINE

LARCH

CEDAR

THE EVERGREENS

The leaves of most of the trees you know, such as Elm, Apple and Catalpa, fall off once a year; that's why autumn is called "fall." These trees are called the Broadleafs. But the Broadleafs are only half the trees in the world. There is another whole set that has leaves as narrow as the needles in a sewing basket. These needle-leaves do not fall off in the fall but stay on all year round, so we call the trees they grow on the Evergreens. The needles are made this way, thin and tough, so the winter winds cannot tear them or the cold freeze them.

In many ways the Evergreens are made differently, because they are much older on earth than the Broadleafs. Some, like Pine, have special tubes inside, with drops of resin in them that squeeze out. Fifty million years ago some insects got stuck in this, and down through the ages it became as clear and hard as glass. Today in museums we can see the insects exactly as they looked then!

LARCH

The needles on LARCH will remind you of water squirting out of a leaky hose. Larch needles look a little like Pine's, but close examining will show that there are many in one bunch, instead of five or less, as Pine has. Larch is the only one of the needle-trees whose needles aren't ever-green. They turn yellow in the fall and fall off, just as the leaves of the Broadleafs do.

The wood of Larch has many good uses. Perhaps your house has some in it, for it is often used as lumber. It is also used for railroad ties — those square logs that hold the tracks in place and that you walk along between the tracks (watching for trains, of course). It is also good for shipbuilding.

Larch is a tree of the Northlands, where it lives in wet or swampy places. The Chippewa Indians named it Tamarack, and now many people know it by that name. They called the long, ropy roots *watap* and used them to sew their birch-bark canoes together.

PINE

The PINE trees are dignified and silent. When one stands in a field or park with only Broadleaf trees nearby, it seems apart from them, and lonely.

But sometimes it grows in a Pine woods with no other kinds of trees, where the forest floor is softly carpeted with dead needles that have fallen off, one by one in the silence, for many years. Anyone walking in a Pine woods only whispers, and the trees whisper, too, in the wind high above.

Pine needles grow in small bundles, each bundle wrapped in Pine tree tissue-paper at the base, especially the new ones at the ends of the twigs. There is always the same number in each bundle on the same tree. Pine trees have the longest needles of any of the Evergreens.

Pine cones are made of wood. Some Mexican Indians comb their hair with them. Sometimes there is sugary, good-smelling resin — pine-sap — stuck on them. The seeds, called pine nuts, are an important food to many people of the world. Often Pines will grow where nothing else will; on rocky mountain

slopes and in dry pastures. Like many other trees, they would give us more gifts, if we gave them a chance and grew them in tree orchards.

Pine trees, very tall, very straight, were once used for masts on sailing ships. Men cut down the biggest ones so there are few giants left. But Pine still has many uses, such as for telephone poles which stand beside country roads and help millions of words buzz across the countryside.

Pine, like Ginkgo, is one of the oldest living kinds of trees. The Pine forests of millions of years ago were silent, too, for most of the animals had no voices. Only the wind could be heard as it blew clouds of golden pollen dust, just as it does today.

The resin has many important uses, such as in the making of turpentine. Woodsmen, finding trees slashed by fierce claws, say that bears were after the resin to rub on their fur!

FIR

It is a Fir tree that has the honor of being our favorite Christmas tree, because its needles stay on longest in a warm house. (Spruce is second best.) To test to be sure that it is a Fir, twist off a needle. It will leave a little round circle on the branch. There is a tiny white dot in the circle. That is the pipeline that went into the needle-leaf.

This favorite Christmas tree is called BALSAM FIR. Most of the other firs in our country grow tremendously big, in the great, dark forests of the Northwest. Balsam Fir must know it is a Christmas tree, because its cones, instead of hanging, sit up straight on the branch, like the fat wax candles used before there were colored electric lights for decoration. Sometimes there is sugary resin on the cones. It is this sticky resin that gives the pungent smell to Balsam Fir that people love so much. "Balsam blisters" on the bark have resin in them, too; it is so pure and clear that scientists use it to see better through their microscopes.

 WHITE RED BLACK

 NORWAY

SPRUCE

SPRUCE needles are almost as sharp and stiff as the needles in a sewing basket. There are so many on a twig, it looks as fat and round as a kitten's tail. There is a good way to find out if an Evergreen is a Spruce. If a needle is twisted off it leaves a little peg on the branch. When all the needles are off, the branch is covered with a strange design.

Spruces are usually pointed trees with wide bottoms, like an old-fashioned skirt. Because of this, some of the snow can slide down the slope and the branches don't break under its weight. On a snowy day a Spruce is like a cozy tent, where the birds can find shelter from the storm.

There are different kinds of Spruce trees, but they are all used to make much of our paper. Red, White and Black Spruces have different sizes of cones. Norway Spruce's needles don't lie down on the twig, but stick out straight, like the bristling tail of a scared cat.

73

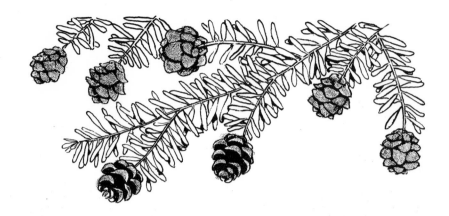

HEMLOCK

Walking among high HEMLOCKS in winter, you can look up at the fairyland of the treetops, with the soft snow piled on the lacework of the branches, while some of it silently sifts through, so as not to weigh them down.

And there are rosebuds in the snow! The great numbers of little cones look like small brown roses, dangling lightly on the tips of the branches.

Even if some Hemlocks grow very large, the needles are smaller than those of Fir or Spruce, and softer. Each needle has two white stripes underneath. A needle crushed in your fingers has the clean smell of the forest. Hemlock tree is graceful and free and lighthearted.

In the spring, new light-green needles grow from the ends of the dark-green branches. Hemlocks make a fairyland all year round.

CEDAR

Cedar needles don't look at all like needles. They are about the size of a pencil point, and pressed close against the twig, which looks very different than all the other Evergreens. The Indians called Cedar *Oo-see-ha-tah*, which means feather-leaf. The word sounds like a small wind blowing.

RED CEDAR is also called Juniper. The wood is red-orange and has a delicious smell. Before the biggest trees were chopped down, cedar-chests and closets were made of it because moths were the only ones who didn't like the smell. Red Cedar has blue berries and two kinds of needles. On young branches are sharp ones like pencil-leads, sticking out; but on older ones the needles are almost too small to see, and the branch feels smooth. The bark is shreddy and ragged. The people of Iceland say Juniper and Mountain Ash are enemies and cannot live in the same house together. But if a ship is made partly of Mountain Ash, they insist that it must have Juniper aboard or it will sink!

SOME VERY STRANGE TREES

As the world's trees parade past, our imaginations are filled with wonder at the endless kinds. We have made friends of the ones that have come down through time to us and others that have crossed oceans to meet us. Let us look far for even stranger ones. Some have no branches, some no trunk and some not a single leaf. One, the Strangler Fig, creeps up another tree and wraps its trunk around it until the supporting tree dies. The Sausage Tree has long sausage fruit hanging from it, but this doesn't taste nearly as good as real sausages! Some weigh more than ten pounds! The Baobab, that lives in Africa, has the elephant of all tree-trunks, but there is not much tree-top to go with it. The inside becomes hollow and stores water, but sometimes small furry animals, lizards and snakes live in it.

But for beauty there is the HOLLY tree. The leaves are shiny and dark green, with sharp points on the edges. Birds love to eat the red berries but they don't admire their beauty as we do. This is one Broadleaf tree that is ever-green all year round. It is most common in the South, but Christmas time finds some in homes across the United States, bright and cheery, as a symbol of Christmas in the cold winter world.

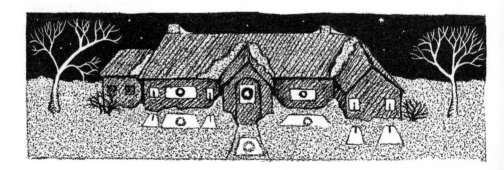

THE CHOCOLATE TREE

Cacao is the real name of this tree, but what better name could it have than the CHOCOLATE TREE?

When America was discovered no one had ever yet tasted a steaming cup of cocoa. The Spanish explorers found the Mexican Indians grinding up some beans into a cold spicy and very special drink they called *chocolatl*. But it was so bitter! The Spanish mixed sugar with it and took the recipe back to Spain, and kept it a secret for one hundred years.

But it was too good to keep secret for much longer. News of it spread, and finally a Frenchman in London mixed milk with the cocoa and sold it in "chocolate houses." It was very expensive and for a long time only wealthy people could afford it.

Today our supplies of chocolate come from the Gold Coast of Africa, Brazil and other hot, moist countries. The bean pods are cut from the trunk and branches with very long-handled knives. The shells are removed, leaving the beans, or "nib," which is mashed and cooked in big kettles to make bitter chocolate. Cocoa and cocoa butter are made from this, and also the sweet chocolate that people enjoy in all parts of the world.

THE RUBBER TREE

When Columbus came to the New World he found the Indians bouncing balls made from tree-sap. The Mexican Indians rubbed the same kind of sap on their capes to make them rainproof. Explorers took some of the strange stuff back to their countries to show people, but could think of nothing to do with it — except bounce it! A historian, who had never seen anything bounce, wrote that the balls acted as if they were alive.

Three hundred years later, an Englishman rubbed a piece of the tree-sap on some paper on which he had been writing, and found that it erased his words! He was the first man to call it rub-ber.

And then automobiles were invented around 1900, and how could millions of wheels roll so quietly over thousands of highways today if there were no rubber tires?

The first big forests of rubber were along the Amazon River in South America. The natives went through the dark jungles, collecting the milky sap from slits in the trees. This "rubber milk" is called latex. It takes great skill to make the slit exactly the right way. The natives prepared it for export by dipping their paddles in the latex and holding them over a fire

78

until it hardened. Then they wrapped more latex over that, like taffy, until the paddles were heavy with it, when they would scrape it off.

More modern methods of collecting it are used today, or not nearly as much rubber could be made as the world needs. In 1950 almost two million tons were used. The largest rubber plantations are in such hot, rainy countries as Malaya, Indonesia and Ceylon. If you can find them on the map, you will see how close to the Equator they are.

Certainly the trees give us no queerer gift than this one that snaps, rolls, erases, bounces and can go tramping through the mud.

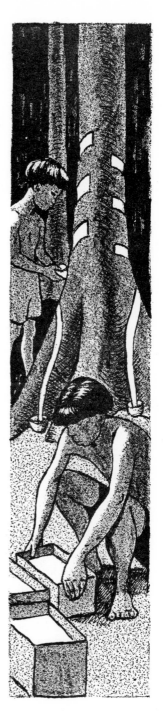

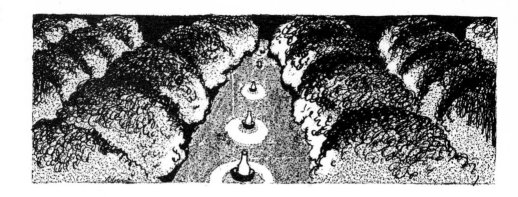

THE CITRUS TREES

Orange — Lemon — Grapefruit — Lime — Tangerine

All these fruits of the sunset colors — orange, yellow, green — are cousins. They not only make a million-dollar industry by growing politely in rows in huge orchards, but they also grow in people's yards in California and Florida, and sometimes wild in the woods.

These fruit trees are a great gift. The people who spoon down a half a grapefruit or swallow orange juice quickly before school, or sip (or sell) lemonade or limeade on a hot summer day, or eat a tangerine on a picnic, should look more closely at what the tree has made them. Inside an orange are hundred of drops of pure juice, each one wrapped in tissue paper, each with a threadlike handle. The drops are bundled into each of the ten segments you find after the peeling is off. Each segment is the right size for two juicy mouthfuls. These fruits are all called citrus fruits, and give us Vitamin C, without which we could not possibly be healthy. The leaves are delicious to smell, especially when one is crushed. They are dark and shiny. If the orchards become even slightly too cold at night, the fruitmen start heaters going between the trees.

BANYAN

BANYAN is the tree with its roots in the air. They grow out of the branches and hang down like snakes, until they reach the ground. Then they burrow into the soil like all good roots should. All these roots growing from the branches look like pillars holding up a leafy roof. One Banyan is so large a whole army once rested under it. Another has 350 large "trunks" and 3,000 smaller ones!

Hundreds of years ago, when Europeans first sailed into India, they found Indian merchants selling their wares under these strange trees. They called the merchants *banians* and then changed the spelling a little to call the trees they sat under "banyans."

Today the Banyans are sacred trees; that is, holy trees, to many of the people of India. They believe that spirits might live in them, and so have special rules to keep anyone from hurting the trees at all. And so they can keep on growing forever, if they wish!

BALD CYPRESS

BALD CYPRESS spends its life standing up to its knees in water. And it does have real knees, only no one would ever guess what they are used for. Cypress breathes through them! Air cannot reach the roots through the soil, as it does in other trees, because they are covered with water, so they must send up woody knobs that not only look like knees but are called that.

Bald Cypress grows nowhere else in the world but a few places in the South and in Mexico. Its home is the swamps and bayous; rivers of "dead water," that do not flow but lie still and dark. Long streamers of Spanish moss hang from the branches like immense cobwebs, swaying slowly and looking like misty, gray-green ghosts. A few families live in cabins perched on dry ground around the bayous. The boys and girls of the family, all of them, must help in the work of finding food: frogs, oysters and crabs, in the water among the Cypress trees.

A strange world to live in!

BANANA

BANANA is the tree with no trunk. At least it has no real trunk, with heartwood and cambium like most trees. Instead, it is made up of the stems of giant leaves that have fallen off. These are nearly the largest tree-leaves in the world, and each time one dies, the stem stays on to make the tree a little higher. The trunk is then hollow all the way up. When it is quite high, a bud starts from the bottom and pushes up through the hollow tube to the very top, and out between the leaves. It grows into a huge bunch of bananas; and when that has been cut off, while still green, and sent away, the whole tree dies. Each tree grows only one bunch of bananas. A new circle of trees shoots up out of the bottom of each dead tree.

Americans have only eaten bananas for a few years. But for centuries people in tropical countries have used the leaves for umbrellas, roofs, sandals, raincoats and sails, and have woven the fibers into clothing, hats, fishnets, mats and baskets. They have fried, boiled, roasted and baked the fruit, ground it into flour for banana-bread and mixed it with nuts. Bananas have kept millions of people alive and better off.

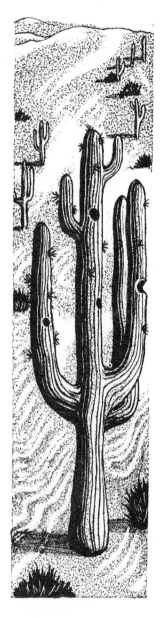

SAGUARO *(Pronounced sa-war-o)*

SAGUARO is the tree with no leaves. It doesn't even look at all like a tree, though it's very tall. It is really a cactus-tree that lives only in the desert of southwestern United States. "Cactus" in Greek means "prickly plant," and anyone who has touched a little cactus in a flower pot knows this is painfully true. The prickers are really Saguaro's leaves. Since the desert is unbelievably hot by day and freezing by night, and fierce winds blow cutting sand across it, anything that grows there must be tough and courageous to stay alive.

Saguaro is a bird skyscraper. Woodpeckers peck holes in it, but only live there one year. The next year they rent them out to flickers, fly-catchers and little cactus wrens to set up housekeeping. When they, too, leave for other homes, owls move in. Because the sun would quickly draw out the valuable water through each new hole that is made, Saguaro builds woody walls around the inside of each one. These are so hard that they have been found on the desert, looking like wooden bowls, long after the rest of Saguaro was dead and gone. But while Saguaro lives it contains these good rooms for birds, and that is why it is the skyscraper of the desert.

84

DATE PALM

The Palm tree is the tree with no branches. DATE PALM has meant life to desert people ever since time began, for in the desert, wherever it grows, it makes a spot of cool shade and is a sign that water is near. Long ago a tree in such a place needed an especially good way to spread its seeds, and so it began to pack sweet, sticky food around them. People and birds came flocking for the fruit and spread the seeds to distant places. Nowadays men carefully plant orchards of Date Palms.

Date Palm looks very different from the trees we know. Because it has no branches and the leaves are so high, little trees can grow underneath— Figs, Apricots and Olives. Dates are easy to pack and carry without spoiling, in swaying camel caravans across the desert. Most of our dates come from Iraq. The desert people grind them into flour for bread and cakes and bake them in brick ovens. They give them to their animals for fodder, and even grind up the seeds to eat. They make offerings of them in their temples.

This gift of the desert is one of the world's most important foods.

COCONUT PALM

If Date Palm lives in the driest places, Coconut Palm lives in the wettest. If Date Palm's seed is small, Coconut Palm's is the largest.

 This tree leans over the water and drops its seeds with a splash. These coconuts are the largest of all seeds. The round, hairy ones we can buy in stores are just the inside; each one once had a big, tough shell around it. After it has floated along the shore or across a stretch of ocean to an island, the outer shell cracks off. Soon a little palm tree pokes out from one of the "eyes" of the giant inner seed. Three spots give this a funny face, like two eyes and a mouth; native children call coconuts "monkey faces." We can poke a hole through the "mouth" and, when the milk pours out, know what the native people love to drink! Boys can make two hard bowls by sawing a coconut in half. We can eat the white meat inside—nothing else tastes quite like it! When dried, the meat is called copra, and butter, oil and wax are made from it. The copra industry is an important one.

SEQUOIA

Trees are the biggest living things in the world, and the oldest. But one tree is even bigger than all the others, and older.

If this tree looked down on the people on the ground they would look like ants to it, as its tips reach up into the sky. Forest fires hardly hurt it. Lightning and thunder are formed in its tops. But it does not let these nuisances bother it; it only continues to live and grow older.

SEQUOIA is as high as a twenty-story office building. A circle of twenty-five boys and girls would just reach around its trunk. An entire village could be built from the lumber of one large tree. Its lowest branches are ten stories above the ground, and sometimes just one branch is bigger than a whole Tulip Tree or Sycamore.

The forests of Sequoia grow only in California and Oregon, where they are bathed in cool ocean fog and warm sunlight. The oldest trees that live there now were hatched from their tiny seeds when civilization was beginning to

grow in Egypt, more than 4,000 years ago; they were already old when Jesus lived, and nearly 1,500 years later when America was discovered they still grew. When Abraham Lincoln was born, white men had not yet discovered the secret, silent Sequoia forests.

But white men became Sequoia's worst enemy, and we hope they will cut no more down. If you hear of Redwood and Big Tree, these are the two kinds of Sequoia.

In 1770 a Cherokee Indian boy was born in Tennessee. It was important then to be able to run as swiftly as a deer, but this lame boy could not do as the others could. Life was hard for the Indians. The white men killed many, burned their homes and drove them from their land toward the West. Hunting was poor in Oklahoma and the other places they camped, and the Indians fought much among themselves and could not understand the ways of the white men who took their land. The lame Indian spent many years inventing a way to write the Cherokee language—his tribesmen thought he was making bad magic, and wanted to kill him. He was an old man before they finally understood how much they needed an alphabet in their own language in order to hold their proud tribe together. He was a great Indian—his name was Sequoya—and our greatest trees were named in his honor.

THE MONEY TREE

Did you ever hear of money growing on trees? Perhaps you can find a MONEY TREE. Its green leaves are papery and have square corners. In fact, they look exactly like dollar bills. The seeds are heavy and shiny and as round as Elm seeds, but larger. They look a lot like dimes and pennies, nickels and quarters.

Everyone wants to find a Money Tree, or thinks he does. He thinks he would buy most of the things in the world with the money, and be happy. But ask anyone who owns most of the things in the world and he'll tell you he's not happy with them.

But ask anyone who IS happy just WHY he is, and he'll tell you he has a secret way. It's this: *he's very interested in something*, or in lots of things. Maybe it's baseball, or model airplanes, or collecting stamps. If you ask a girl, maybe its because she loves swimming, or designing doll clothes, or singing, or just making the house look nice. All these people know there isn't any such thing as the Money Tree, and they don't even care.

And a lot of people get a lot of happiness out of looking at trees everywhere they go, and thinking about how they grow, and learning their names. Knowledge of trees would be useful to them, too, if they should ever get lost in the woods. And it doesn't cost them a penny!

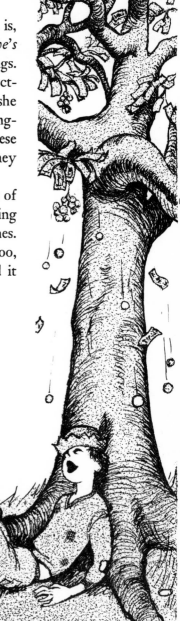

INDEX